PIONEER VALLEY EDUCATIONAL PRESS, INC

AMERICAN FERRIES

MICHÈLE DUFRESNE

TABLE OF CONTENTS

Early Ferries 8
Foot Ferries... 10
Auto Ferries 12
Double-Ended Ferries 14
Glossary/Index 20

Have you ever taken a ride on a ferry? Before trains, steamboats, cars, and trucks, ferries were the best method of **transportation**. Ferries carried **passengers**, animals, and food across rivers, lakes, and other waterways.

➤ A ferry is a boat used to carry passengers, vehicles, and cargo across water.

3

Today, there are many different ways to get across rivers, lakes, and other waterways, but ferries still provide transportation in some places.

▶ Ocracoke Island Ferry, Outer Banks, NC

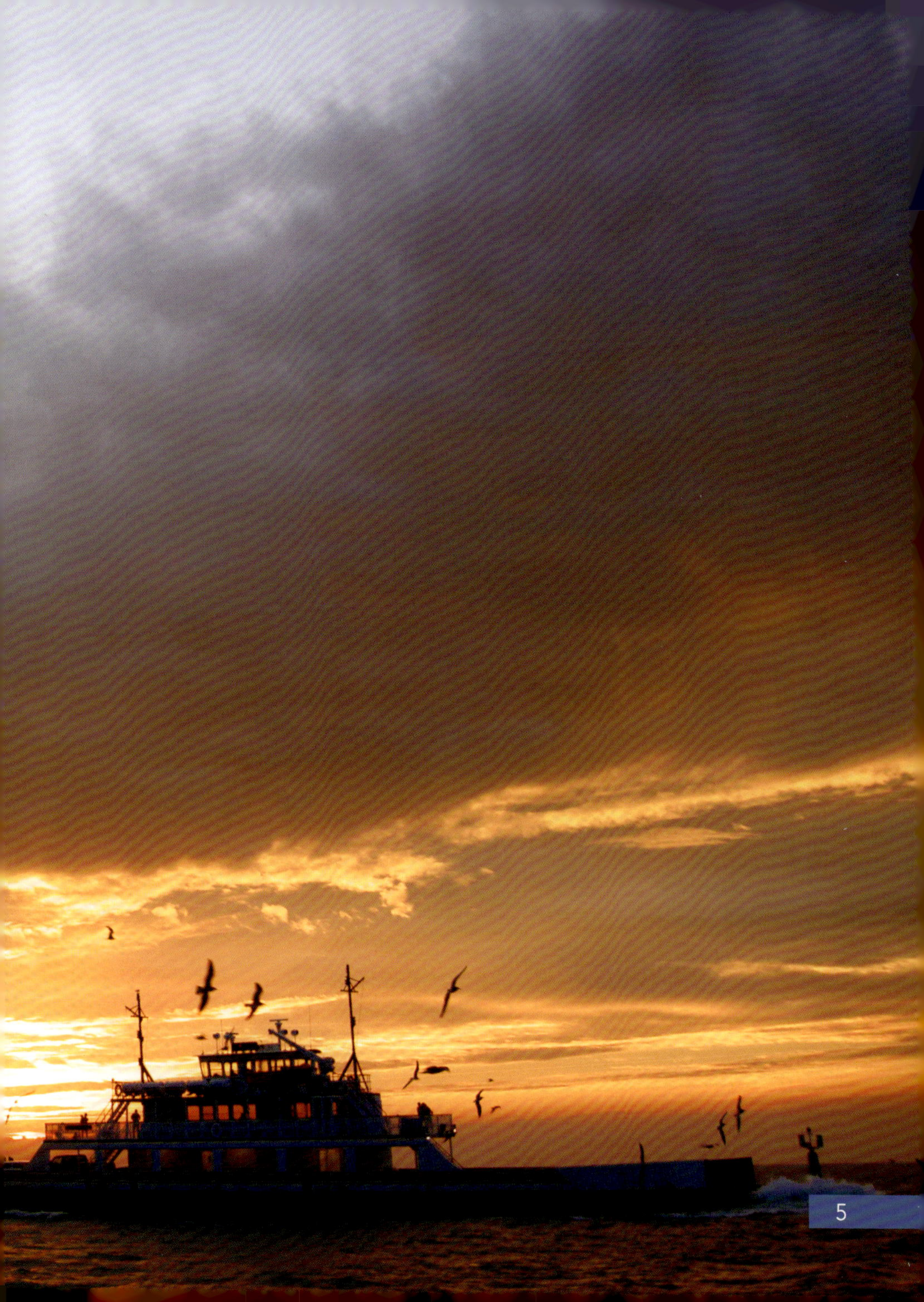

Along the coast of North Carolina there are many small islands. An easy way to travel from one island to the next is to hop on a ferry that runs between the islands. You will see many beautiful sights along the way.

▼ Ferry boat heading into channel on Bald Head Island, North Carolina.

EARLY FERRIES

The first ferries were very different from most of the ferries in use today. The first ferry was a small raft that carried passengers across a river. A person pushed the raft with a pole.

Later, ferries were powered by horses on treadmills or by steam engines.

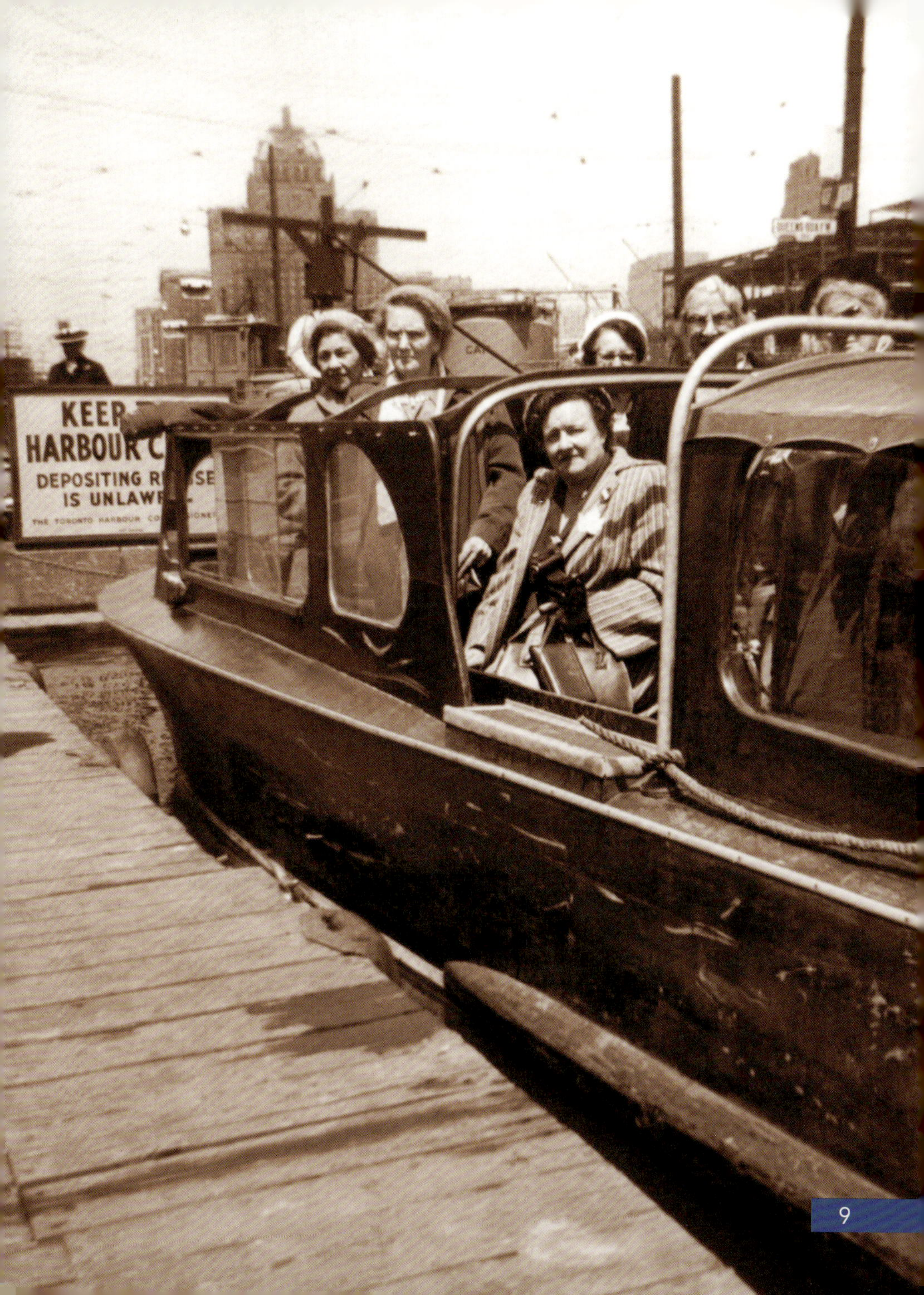
HARBOUR
DEPOSITING
IS

FOOT FERRIES

A ferry that is just for people or bicycles is called a foot ferry. These ferries usually travel only a short distance.

11

AUTO FERRIES

Early ferries carried horses and wagons across water. Auto ferries are used today to transport cars and other vehicles, as well as, passengers across water.

13

DOUBLE-ENDED FERRIES

Some ferries have a front and back that are the same. This allows the ferry to **shuttle** back and forth between two places without turning around.

▸ The double-ended Washington State Ferry is the most used ferry system in the world.

15

The Staten Island Ferry
in New York City
is a double-ended ferry.
This ferry has been taking passengers
back and forth between
Manhattan and Staten Island
for many years.
It carries over 21 million passengers
back and forth each year.
The five-mile journey
takes 25 minutes each way.

Riding the Staten Island Ferry is a favorite activity for tourists. You can see the Statue of Liberty and views of New York City as you travel.

Although not as many people use ferries today,
they still provide important transportation.
Ferries can save driving time and can also be
an enjoyable way to travel.

▲ Staten Island Ferry

GLOSSARY

passengers: people that travel

shuttle: to move back and forth

transportation: a way of traveling from one place to another

INDEX

cable 10
cars 2, 12
foot ferries 10
operation 6
passengers 2, 8, 12, 16

shuttle 14
Staten Island 16-17, 18
transportation 2, 4, 18
travel 10, 17, 18,
waterways 2, 4